(Chapter 1)

(Suffering)

In life we will learn nothing is fair as we go along life's journey. To stay strong was what I was already told by the age of 5 years old. That the world eats the weak and spits them out like they are nothing. Less than trash thrown out to the curb to be carried off and just thrown away. To stay strong through all of life's tests and obstacles.

Life the struggle to succeed and thrive and to make it to another day. That's how I always defined life from a kid on through adulthood. Growing up wasn't easy, we lived a poor life. We struggled just to eat most nights. Most nights we went to bed without dinner. Our bellies would grumble and roar in pain. I remember it all to well. As if it were yesterday.

And it would never get any easier for us. All 5 of us children. We just couldn't break away from the poorness life had promised to bestow on us or so it seemed. And as far as we knew that was how we

were supposed to live. My mother didn't know any better. She had met my dad and got married as a
child her self at the age of 16 my father was only 17 at the time.

Promised a world of happiness she was suckered into a world of torture. She hadn't noticed yet but she
was about to find out for sure. The next 50 years would be hell. Wanting in one hand and shitting in the
other would be the phrase used. And also pave the road that life would take her down. As she traveled
on her journey.

Growing up in the county of Barboursville Kentucky was a rough way of life in the early 1950's. A young
woman growing up didn't have much to look forward too back in those days. Having to cook and sew for
chores was the daily ordeal. If one were caught slacking they would have to go out and pick a switch.
And if it broke another one would be sought after.

That was the life the country way of living. My mother grew up in a life of chaos and hell with her sister Shirley. At the age of 13 they were pulled from their home when their mother had killed her husband. As she had walked in and caught him sexually assaulting her in their own damn bedroom. It was in that moment she had went into the kitchen grabbing a butcher knife and walked back into the bedroom.

The man continued with his assault. As my Grandmother now stood directly behind him. As he went to slap his own daughter yet once again. She had raised the knife up and over her head as she brought it down into his neck in full wrath at this moment. The knife now penetrating into her sick husband's body as he suddenly shook in pain and with much suffering. Blood now poured out of him immensely.

(Chapter 2)

(Massacre)

It was in that moment he fell off of his daughter and onto the floor. He was now bleeding immensely from his neck as the poor mother told her daughter to hurry up and grab her clothes and to leave the room. The girl listened as she sprung up from the bed and reached out to the chair grabbing her belongings. Immediately running for the door as she yanked it open and then slammed it back behind her.

She stood their in the hallway corridor. As she waited to hear what would happen next. Suddenly she heard a scream and then that was followed by several more screams afterwards. She could hear the knife being slammed into her sick father's body as her mother destroyed any life that was left from within him. And then after a minute which seemed like a life time. It was silent but it was finished and over with.

My grandmother had blacked out in that moment. And when she'd came to she would realize that she had stabbed her own husband over 25 times. Killing him with overkill. Sure he got what he'd deserved but in the end. My grandmother would receive over 20 years in the Marysville Correctional Prison in Ohio for women. She never complained not one time. She never looked back nor did she ever regret killing him.

After 20 years she was released and had moved back to Barboursville Kentucky and settled down with a new man Challis. My new papaw treated us very well. But my grandmother never treated any of us good after that time had gone by. She had been totally transformed by having spent so many years in custody and as well the property of the state of Ohio Department Of Rehabilitation And Corrections.

We all thought that the years of being imprisoned had just ruined her as a person. And that she couldn't ever recover from the pain and torment she'd suffered for years. We went to visit her and the visit was horrible. She would end up pulling a belt and a knife out on me Calling me a liar. As she started to come my way slowly but surely. Her eyes changing instantly into a deeper darker color the rage had showed itself once more.

We had to get out of their fast after that incident had happened. It appeared that my grandmother was going to try to hurt me with either the knife or the belt or both. My mother wasn't about to take any chances so we were on the next bus going to Cincinnati, Ohio once again heading home. Totally surprised by her actions we were in fear for our lives.

(Chapter 3)

(FEAR)

My mother wasn't putting her kids in danger like that. Her mother had totally flipped out on me for nothing. Instantly we knew there was a problem with Grandma. That wasn't like her to act that way towards me. She had clearly lost her mind at that point in time and had to be placed somewhere and fast. What was needed as I had told my mother was most likely medicine to control her anger.

She was diagnosed and placed at Waverly Hills Sanatorium down in Louisville Kentucky. Upon arriving there. She was treated horribly by the staff. For a while at least until they found out directly who she was. Then once that had happened she was treated fairly and left alone. The treatment plan was started and in the end had really helped her in many ways control her madness.

After all the woman had witnessed her own daughter being sexually molested. She had murdered her own husband. She had stabbed him 28 times in all. But in many people's eyes it was justifiable and totally correct what she had done. The husband had committed the most brutal acts of violence one could ever imagine. My mother's mother had seen some shit in her days. But nothing ever of that nature.

It was at that moment my grandmother had clearly lost her mind. Seeing what she had seen had hit her like a ton of bricks. Not able to believe that her own husband had done this to their daughter. Costing her a life of any kind that would be considered normal. The most significant of skills in survival she would be forced to learn along her life's journey.

This ordeal had caused a whole whirlwind of sadness. Throughout the whole family. No one was ever the same Gain. Especially Ellen my grandmother. God bless her soul. She was put into a situation that nobody could honestly say. They wouldn't have done the very same thing she had done during that moment in time.

Anyone in their right frame of mind would have done the same thing I do believe. To walk in and find a husband and a father as well. Abusing his own children. When he's supposed to protect them. But had done the exact opposite. Betraying the whole families trust instead. What does one do. How do you handle that kind of betrayal and brutality ?

(Chapter 4)

(Stripped)

 After all the girls were each and every one taken from their homes. Placing all of them into foster care. It was a horrible time for these young women. They would all end up running away from their homes. As they would try as hard as possible to make it through this cruel world all alone. Not having anyone to rely upon for help in any way what so ever.

And they would all struggle each and everyone of them. They would have life so hard. My moms half sister would run off to Colorado and get married. Her sister Sheila would run off to Michigan and get married as well. And my Uncle June bug would also move off to Michigan as well and start his own life in Ann Arbor Michigan.

Years would go by and no contact would happen between any of them. And then out of nowhere over a period of several years each and every family member would show up at our doorstep some years later down the road. After her family members had all established a life of their own. They had started to miss each other dearly.

Finally coming into our lives was little Cheyenne. She was only 5 years old and clearly lacked any kind of communication skills for a child her age. She had without a doubt been treated badly in her years as a child as well. The poor kid had been living in Colorado and had been tormented and also abused as well in many ways. We would find that out a little later on down the road.

Mentally we knew for sure she had been abused. So upon their arrival Dorothy would take her to the doctors office for a Checkup. And then it was finally confirmed that Cheyenne had been sexually abused as well by someone. Later after a set of thorough investigations by the police it was discovered that her father had been found to be the one who was molesting the poor child.

(Chapter 5)

(Confronted)

Dorothy totally flipped out and confronted her sister after she'd found out just what had happened. Cheyenne had been tormented by her own father Mark. For many years she had suffered horribly. It was then Dorothy had made sure Cheyenne would not have to go back to that hell hole ever again. Eventually it would be known that Shirley clearly had no clue of what had been going on.

She threw her sister out and told her to not come back. But she would come back pregnant a year later and hooked on Alcohol and Crack. Dorothy would allow her to live under her roof once again but only by a set of strict rules. And if they weren't followed then she'd have to leave and never be allowed to return again. She didn't want her sister setting bad examples.

Shirley would often run off and play her games now that Cheyenne was gone. And Away from the danger her mother had been responsible for. Shirley was bad at this point. Heavy drinking and drugging was her pain killer. And she'd stay so messed up that she couldn't function as a human being. She was clearly a lost soul.

Dorothy had felt so badly about Shirley carrying on the way she was. But after all. Shirley had been being raped by her own damn father for many years. The poor woman was trying to kill the pain inside. She had been molested and even after the fact. had watched her own father get killed. Being stabbed to death repeatedly very many times.

The woman would never be the same ever again after that. And that was the part everyone wasn't thinking about. Dorothy was though. That's why she gave her so much room for error. Trying to give Shirley the room to heal. But she never would fully get back to normal. She was damaged goods Inside and out. All the way to the center of her core.

Shirley had gone through her whole pregnancy using and abusing. When Ashley was finally born it was a blessing in disguise. It would give her new hope. But she would also mess that situation up as well. Ashley was born immediately going through withdrawal. Which was very dangerous for a new born to have to suffer through.

(Chapter 6)

(The Adoption)

The doctors tried to make her as comfortable as possible. But it was all they could do for the poor little baby. The plan being to make her as comfortable as possible. The rest she'd have to fight through herself as an infant. She was immediately adopted by Dorothy. And she would shortly send Shirley back to Colorado once again. Away from the family for the welfare of the child.

Time would pass and Ashley would fight for her life so sick from the drugs that she'd been passed along to her during her mother's pregnancy. She'd have a couple Surgeries to help her heal. But during one procedure the poor child had flat lined completely during the operation. It took several minutes to bring her back to life. She was a very sick child.

She had died right their on the operating table. The poor kid was so sick from all of the Alcohol and Crack Cocaine her mother had consumed during her pregnancy with her. It was by some miracle from the Lord. That the doctors were able to bring the sick girl back to life. She was blessed by God that day. I still believe that to this very day 25 years later.

She would survive the operation but would suffer for years and years to come from the side effects of the party life her mother had lived while pregnant. It would affect the child's school work. She would make straight F's on her report cards. She couldn't get along with others. Social anxiety disorder and many other disorders as well she would suffer from.

Her whole life was hell from a child on through to adult hood. So many secrets were held back from the child as well. Just so she could live a normal life as possible. Over the years Ashley would put two and two together and figure it all out. She knew she had a different mother out there in the world somewhere. And that fact alone would keep her curious.

She would later contact her and try to build a relationship with her mother. But it would be only in her time of need that she would even attempt to try to contact her. Their mother daughter relationship was doomed from the start. Nothing could ever fix the betrayal Shirley had placed upon her own daughter. It would take years before they would ever even try to fix the damage that had been done.

(Chapter 7)

(Pain)

Later in life as the child developed into an adult there was so much pain it couldn't be over come. And she would live a life of struggle. Poorness and torment. Losing loved one after another she would have a 50/50 chance of ever recovering from it all. She would make some progress over the years. As she fought through the pain and anguish.

She would then get to meet her grandmother shortly before she passed away. Ellen Howard was released from Marysville women's prison in the early 90's after serving a 20 year prison sentence for Murder. She had been found responsible for her husband's death. She didn't receive a fair trial at all from the local court system. They would use her as an example for other battered women in which that was proven to be totally wrong.

Even though he'd been caught raping his own teenage daughter. In which he had been doing it a long while. Ellen was at work at the local saloon. And had been working there for years to make ends meet. I was so glad to hear he was caught finally and had paid for his crimes. He had got what he'd deserved was the opinion of my whole entire family.

It may haven't been by a court of law but the country folks had always handled things a little bit differently back then. Taking the law into their own hands when need be. And in a case like this I knew it'd be this way. It was only fitting what had happened to the man who'd been caught doing the most unthinkable thing to his own kin.

Most of the city had said that she did not deserve to do even one day in jail. After she'd walked in on what she'd seen that night. But the law seen it differently and had no choice but to punish her for her actions. After all the law is the law. Everyone knew she'd been thrown under the bus. Labeled guilty right off of the bat. Not even receiving a fair trial in the due process of her conviction.

(Chapter 8)

(Chances)

If she hadn't of killed him that night much worse may have ended up happening to her. But in the end it played itself out and she'd be stuck doing 20 years. It was far from fair. That's when I knew the law was nothing but a shit storm. And would never trust it again myself. I had learned when it came to the court system. Money talked and bullshit walked, that was just the way it was.

She ended up doing her whole 20 year bit. And would be released in time to see her last grand child born before her death. Upon being released back out into the real world. She had met a man named Challis. A good hard working man who worked down deep in the coal mines of Kentucky. He loved her dearly and she was happy for a while.

Ellen and Challis had started to build a life together after they'd met. And years would go by without any visits. Ellen would save every single disability check she'd ever receive. And stash the money all through out the house. Even in old pillow sacks they would stuff money. Keeping it hidden from his own kids.

Then years later down the road Dorothy would get a call that her mother was ill. Dorothy and Shirley would take off and head down south from Cincinnati Ohio. Going home together for the first time in over 20 years. As sisters they were thrilled to once be together. And they would be back under the sea roof as their mother.

But once upon their arrival they'd be shell shocked by what they'd learned while being away. Outside of the house were 4 dog cages each containing a pit bull. The dogs were healthy but filthy not cared for by Challis as he worked sun up until sundown on many things other than caring for his wife or his pets.

(Chapter 9)

(Neglected)

As the two girls walked into the first floor they find their mother lying in pure filth. Empty food boxes and news papers were allover the floors. The house smelled of urine new and old through out the entire house. Their mother had contracted a body full of bed sores. And they'd become badly infected and had also entered into her blood stream as well.

They went together into the bathroom and gathered a quick plan to get their mother out of the house. After that they planned to clean the house up. They made Challis go get cleaning supplies from the store. And the big cleanup began. As soon as he'd walk out the door the plan would be set into motion. They would make the call for help.

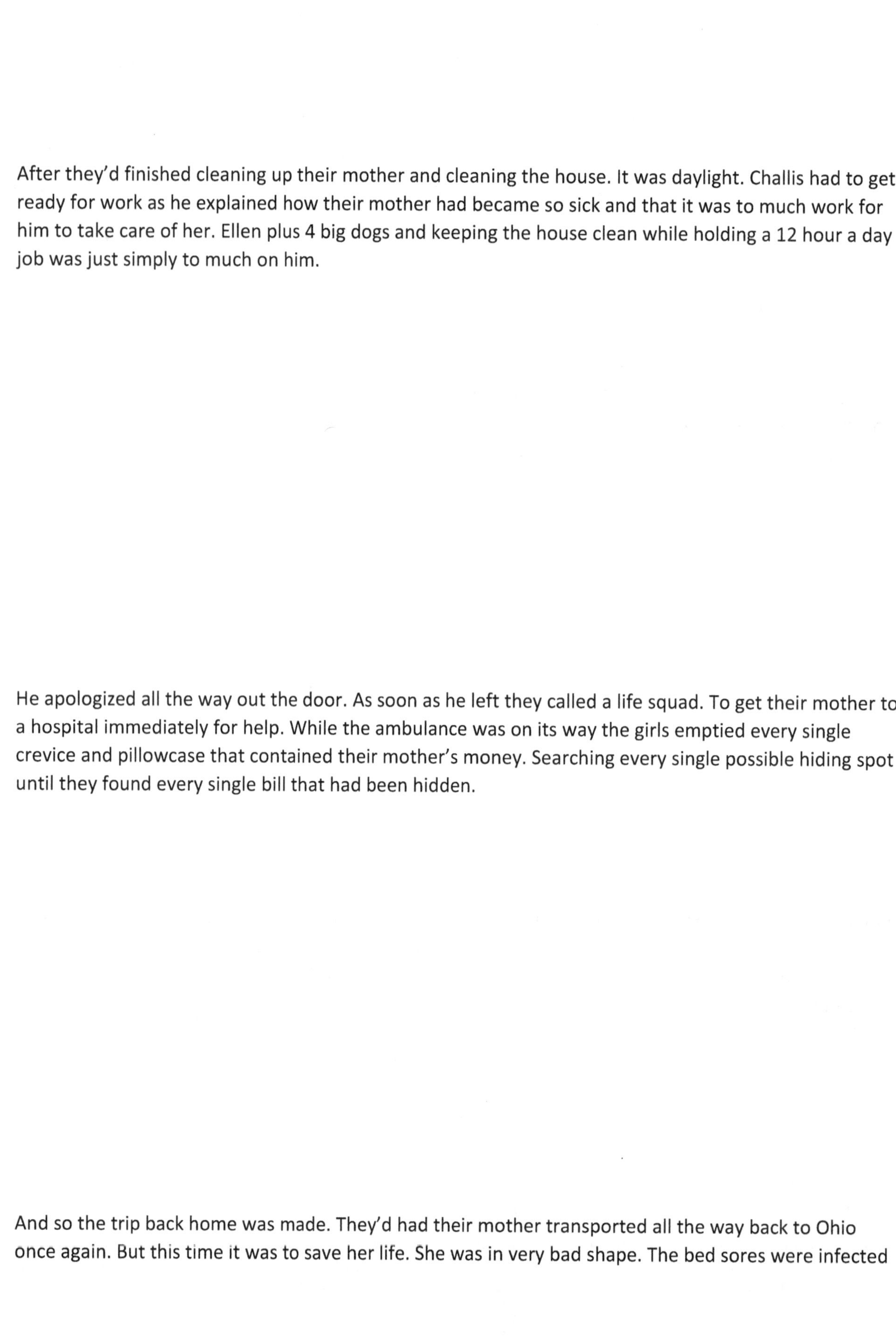

After they'd finished cleaning up their mother and cleaning the house. It was daylight. Challis had to get ready for work as he explained how their mother had became so sick and that it was to much work for him to take care of her. Ellen plus 4 big dogs and keeping the house clean while holding a 12 hour a day job was just simply to much on him.

He apologized all the way out the door. As soon as he left they called a life squad. To get their mother to a hospital immediately for help. While the ambulance was on its way the girls emptied every single crevice and pillowcase that contained their mother's money. Searching every single possible hiding spot until they found every single bill that had been hidden.

And so the trip back home was made. They'd had their mother transported all the way back to Ohio once again. But this time it was to save her life. She was in very bad shape. The bed sores were infected and the infection had entered their mother's blood system. Making for a very critical situation. Life threatening if they didn't get her to a hospital very soon.

(Chapter 10)

(Survival)

She was now in the middle of a heavyweight fight for survival. With antibiotics and bags of medicine as well that had been inserted into an IV and into her body for hydration. She fought for a couple weeks in order to survive. But would end up losing her battle for life on a Sunday evening. I will never forget that phone call.

It killed Dorothy and Shirley to lose their mother. One who'd fought so hard to give them a descent life so long ago only to be stripped of her dignity and pride for killing a sick demented rapist. A man so sick he'd of definitely done it again. What was done had to be done or the situation would have continued for years most likely.

So she did what she felt was right at that particular moment in time. And in the end the choice would betray her as well. Taking what was left of a life from her. Placing her in a women's prison for so long. It took whatever there was of a woman that was left inside of her and had taken it away for good.

The woman was given at least a proper ceremony on her way out. It tore my mother Dorothy to pieces she had always loved her mother so much. I guess because she fought so hard to give her a life during the hard times of the depression. She never quit on her children. She stuck by her family through the tough times. Doing whatever was necessary to survive.

She went above and beyond what was needed to make sure my mother had what she needed to succeed. To not have to live a life of being poor. Having nothing to eat nor anything to drink. She kept Dorothy and Shirley from living a life of hell deep down in the country hills of Barboursville Kentucky.

(Chapter 11)

(Home)

They would take Ellen back to Kentucky and bury her down home. While they were away I had gone to jail for fighting with my father. Drinking got out of hand one night and a fight broke out at the house. I ended up going to jail being charged with domestic violence. My bond was paid soon after I'd arrived and I would be released soon there after.

I remember as I was getting out they were laying my grandmother to rest at that same moment. As I was on my way home. There was a moment that had flashed back to me. It was when we'd first met so many years ago. She'd seemed like such a good woman to me upon first meeting her. But then changing so quickly her mental status.

Just trying to make it in a world gone bad. It was a sad day Id have to say. My mother's other sister would soon visit us after the passing of Ellen. She'd made the trip from Northern Michigan to see us all. And upon arriving we'd learn she also had troubles too. Struggling through so many things in life.

We just guessed that being brought up how they were was just to tough on them all. She was an alcoholic as well drinking daily until she couldn't no longer walk. She'd fall all over the house. A huge embarrassing moment for her sister Dorothy. She couldn't even look at her after the incident had happened.

Charlie would be put on a bus back home to Michigan shortly there after. A few weeks later. Dorothy would get a call from her only brother. June bug was his nickname. He was a successful auto dealer up in Ann Arbor Michigan. He told my mother directly it was a mistake to allow either of them into her life again. That the two of them would only bring trouble.

Dorothy interrupted the conversation with I had to give it a chance for the kids sake. Just like that they had came and gone. That fast it was over. A lifetime of memories had came and gone that quickly. It left Dorothy very depressed. She gave up hope on her siblings after that phone call between her and her brother. For the most part, she would still give them a chance to redeem themselves.

(Chapter 12)

(Losses)

Having to put up with hell and torment all of her life. Dorothy had to go through so much pain in life. To have had a father murdered by her mother. She would go through so much adversity in life. To be put through so much at such an early age she seemed to recover well. She wasn't anything like the others. She was full of fight and had a strong will.

By the age of 15 she would run away from the foster home. She would meet my father and they would hit it off and get married by the age of 16. Falling like a ton of bricks for Jeff Lilly. She would be pregnant by the age of 17. And would start off her marriage with a set of twins. But at that time the doctors hadn't a clue she were carrying identical twins.

The first of the children were well on the way and married she was finally happy for the first time in life. But that's as far as she'd get. Having kids would be the only enjoyment she'd get out of life. Nor would her sisters. They would all live a cursed life or so it would seem. For very many years their wouldn't seem to be very much happiness in their lives.

Shirley was stuck in a world of alcohol and drugs running from one man to another. She was miserable through and through. What had happened to her had severely torn her life apart. She could never get passed it. Hell who could ? Honestly it was as bad a situation for one to have been put through at such an early age in life.

The poor child abused mentally and physically and also sexually. She was actually lucky that worse hadn't happened to her. She was still only a teenager. That is what probably saved her life. It was all God's will what had happened to her. And how it all ended as well was God's plan for her life also. It seemed horrible but in the end it made her tough as nails.

(Chapter 13)

(Paths)

It was a plan that he had placed out for her life. That's what Dorothy had always told her. It was the path that just had to be followed. There was no turning back what was done was done. She had told Shirley you'll only heal once you accept it and just move on forward your life. Only then will you be at peace with it all in your soul.

But they all knew it was way more than that. This was definitely a life changing ordeal that Shirley had gone through. My mother was just trying to boost her moral. Trying to Jumpstart Shirley's life. But the pain that she had suffered was just to much to bare. She just couldn't seem to get passed all that had happened to her.

Her mother Ellen's death had sent her over the edge. She just gave up hope. So fast that it seemed to happen overnight. Shirley was slipping further into depression. There seemed to be only one way to go with it all.. We all thought it would be by way of drugs and or alcohol or both that would take her life away in the end.

But it wasn't that way at all. Shirley had a plan all along. Her own way to live and die by the sword. No one would know just how she'd planned to go. God willing it wouldn't be any other way but hers. Things would set themselves in motion sooner than later. And would surprise us all in the very end.

First off the plan was to make sure that Mark her ex boyfriend would get what was coming to him sooner than later. And then only then could she move forward. So they gathered copies of the doctors reports and then the two of them would set out for Colorado. Shirley had set it all up perfectly.

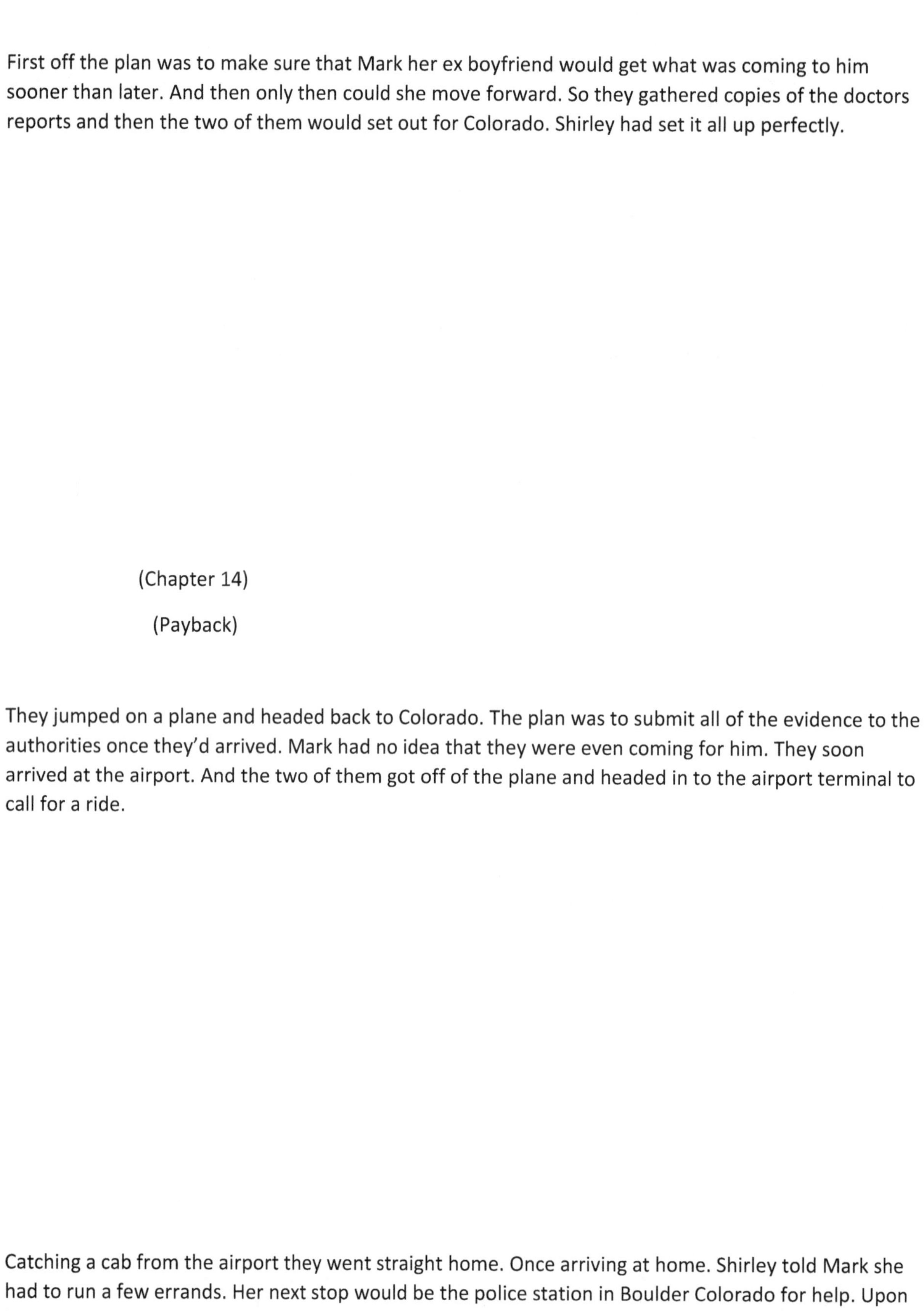

(Chapter 14)

(Payback)

They jumped on a plane and headed back to Colorado. The plan was to submit all of the evidence to the authorities once they'd arrived. Mark had no idea that they were even coming for him. They soon arrived at the airport. And the two of them got off of the plane and headed in to the airport terminal to call for a ride.

Catching a cab from the airport they went straight home. Once arriving at home. Shirley told Mark she had to run a few errands. Her next stop would be the police station in Boulder Colorado for help. Upon her arrival they'd shown the local police the evidence from the doctor reports. They immediately put out a warrant for Mark's arrest.

Shortly after the police set out to try and pick him up on the warrant. In which they were able to do so quickly. Mark was shocked upon their arrival but gave up easily. So that was the end of that chapter as Shirley had wanted it to be. Now "I can start my life over fresh and new" she told herself. "A whole new life and I will build without a man" she said.

But she was never able to start over fresh and new. The hauntings of her past had always came back into her mind slowly crawling in as she was in constant agony. Never being able to fully clear her mind of her past it weighed on her heavily. And so often that she couldn't battle the urges to just wipe it all clean. By way of the bottle as usual.

The alcohol and drugs taking over once again. Slowly consuming her yet again. The poor thing had been through it all no wonder she couldn't escape it all. It was just to much for one person to be able to deal with it all. Shirley would go back to Cincinnati but after dating a family friend for a while. She'd end up back in Colorado again.

(Chapter 15)

(tragedies)

Shortly after Shirley had left back for Colorado to try to start over again. Life would settle down once and for all. There was normality once again at home. No drunks running and falling about the house. Busting their heads or breaking limbs and bleeding about as well. She had finally found just a little bit of peace again in her life.

If only for a little while at least. Not until Jason had learned Renee was cheating on him. She had come over to see him and shortly after started playing her usual head games with him. It weren't nothing new. Other than hinting about the next new man that she was probably entertaining.

Renee had came completely clean all of a sudden. And had told him that she had cheated on him. Jason Immediately grabbed his 22 pistol and put it to his head. Renee continued to tell Jason all of the details of that night. He then stuck the gun into his mouth and as he did the gun went off accidently.

There was blood all over the room Jason was instantly in shock. He found himself running up the basement stairs for help as he came to his senses once again. Dorothy called 911 automatically upon seeing him injured. Awaiting the ambulance towels were broke out to keep him from bleeding so much. Pressure was applied heavily to keep the blood from pouring out.

They compressed a towel inside of his mouth to stop the bleeding from the inside as well. The ambulance finally showed up and they got him stable and took him to UC Hospital for help. The emergency room was full so that it took them several minutes to get him in the door so they waited. Once inside the doctors looked him over. To check the damage that had been done.

In the end there was nothing they could do but let the wound heal and send Jason home. And ordering complete bed rest so the injury could heal up. The bullet would have to fester out on its own. So upon release he would stay with his older brother. So he could be taken care of and also watched in case of another mind fail on his part.

(Chapter 16)

(Death)

As he healed up the wound began to heal slowly but surely. More tragic news would arrive. Charlie had been found at the edge of the woods of her home in Ann Arbor Michigan dead. She had got intoxicated and wandered about until her body shut down from hypothermia. She was so numb she really hadn't felt much at all.

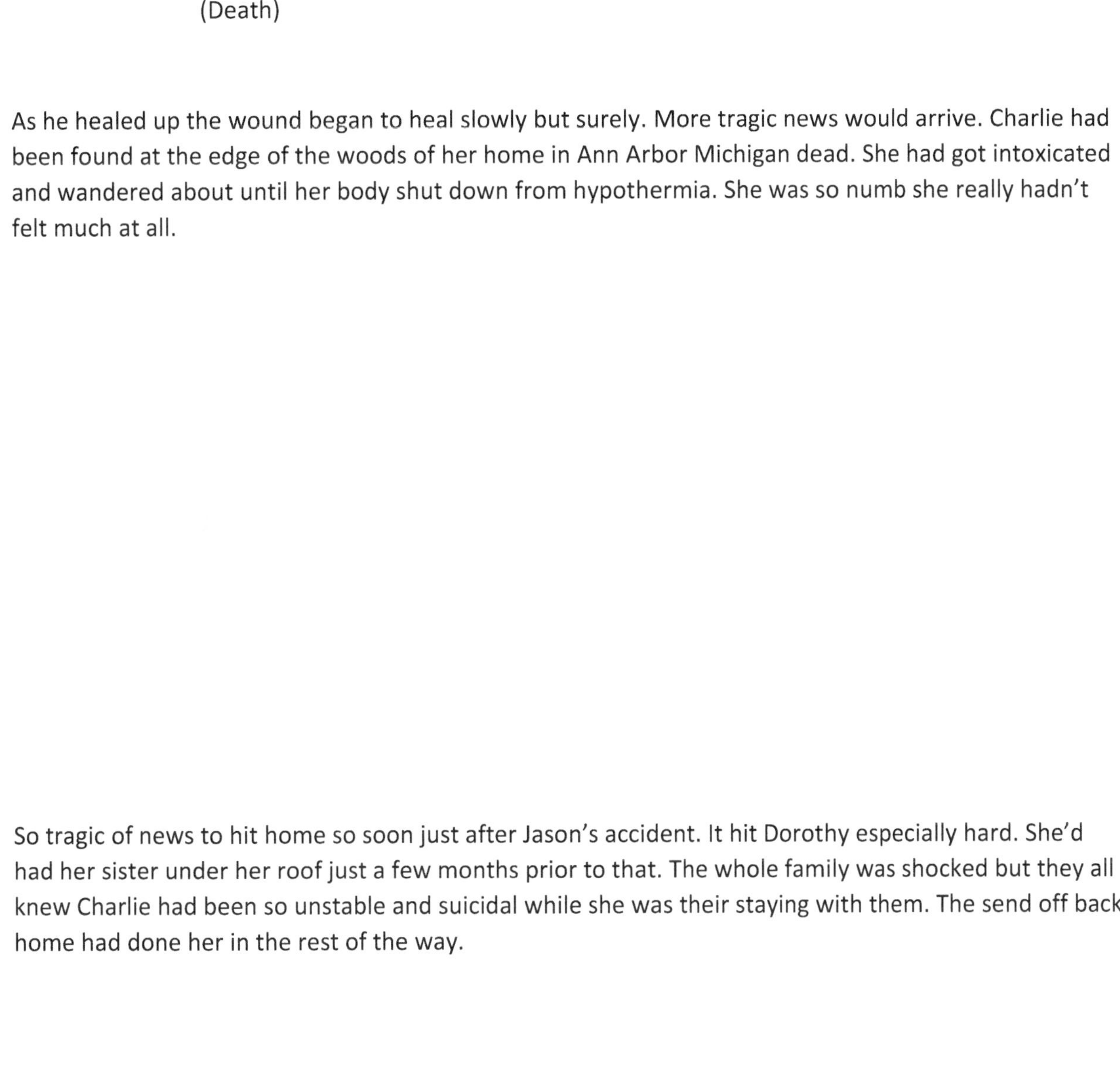

So tragic of news to hit home so soon just after Jason's accident. It hit Dorothy especially hard. She'd had her sister under her roof just a few months prior to that. The whole family was shocked but they all knew Charlie had been so unstable and suicidal while she was their staying with them. The send off back home had done her in the rest of the way.

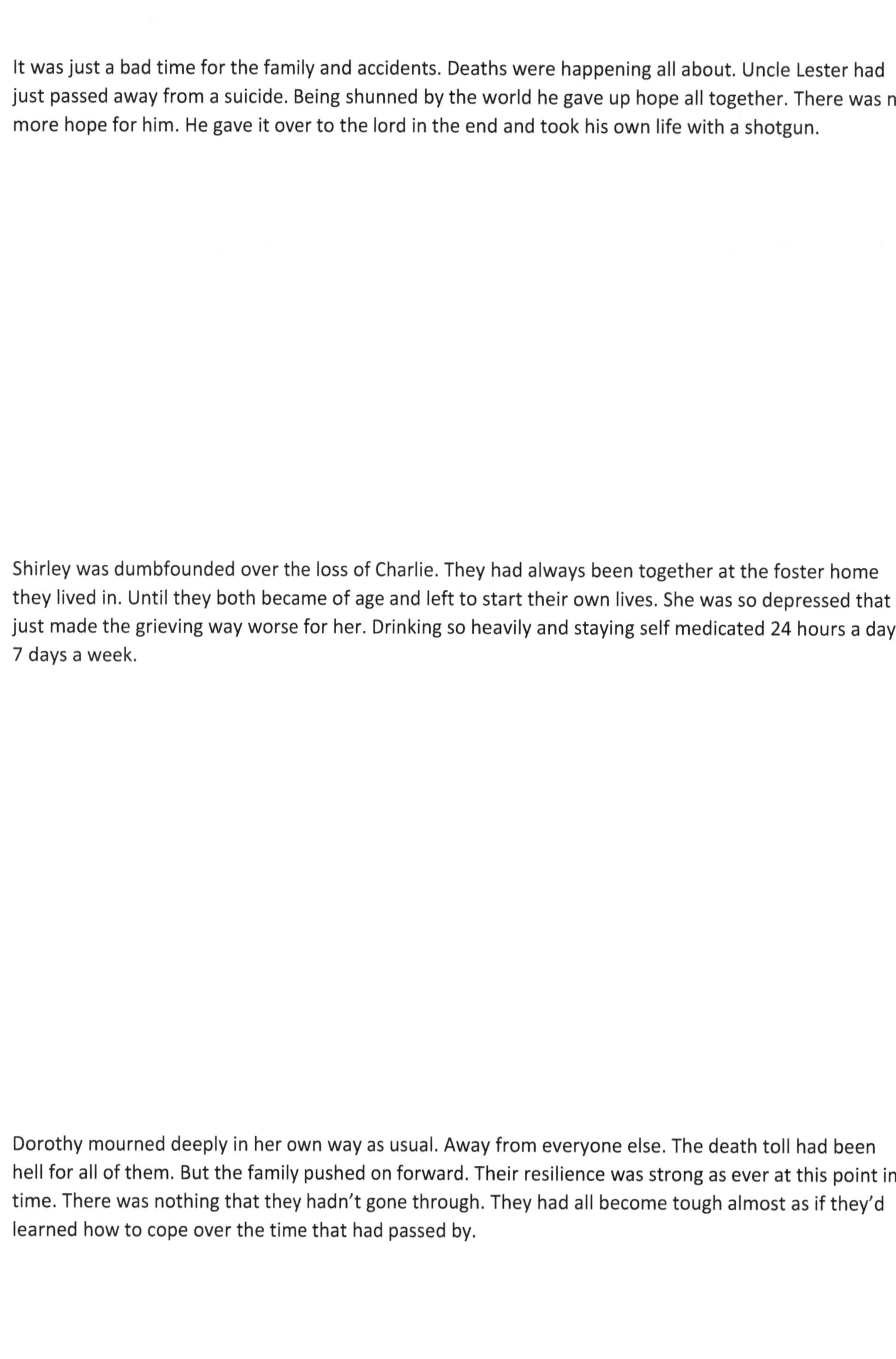

It was just a bad time for the family and accidents. Deaths were happening all about. Uncle Lester had just passed away from a suicide. Being shunned by the world he gave up hope all together. There was no more hope for him. He gave it over to the lord in the end and took his own life with a shotgun.

Shirley was dumbfounded over the loss of Charlie. They had always been together at the foster home they lived in. Until they both became of age and left to start their own lives. She was so depressed that it just made the grieving way worse for her. Drinking so heavily and staying self medicated 24 hours a day 7 days a week.

Dorothy mourned deeply in her own way as usual. Away from everyone else. The death toll had been hell for all of them. But the family pushed on forward. Their resilience was strong as ever at this point in time. There was nothing that they hadn't gone through. They had all become tough almost as if they'd learned how to cope over the time that had passed by.

It felt as if the death would continue to hit the family as if it were a curse set upon them all. The only way to live for them was in the moment and to just love one another. Hoping and praying that it would all just stop at some point. But it wouldn't. The deaths would continue on over the years. Haunting each and everyone of the family members.

(Chapter 17)

(Humbled)

Humbled by death the family just tried to live a normal life. Every test that came along the way they took it head on. No dodging no going around the obstacles that lay before them. They pushed forward through it all gaining toughness and determination along their way. Loving each other as family should. And by just being their for each other.

The kids had all grown up at this point in time. Angie had moved away and started her own family. I had moved on and was currently living a life of wildness. Drinking heavily in the bars and doing drugs with the crew of people I hung around with for the past 20 years or so. Living like a bunch of wild maniacs day in and day out.

Knowing my grandmother had been sentenced to prison for 20 years was a secret that I'd kept for a very long time. But I also agreed with how she handled the situation. That was why I'd never told any of friends. I'm not sure how I would have acted if that had been myself in her shoes. Even though I feel like I would have done the same exact thing.

There is no doubt about it actually. The way in which the man who committed these crimes had acted so ruthlessly for such a long period of time. He deserved to get what he got. Just wish it would have happened sooner than it did. The man deserved everything he got that day. It put an end to a tragedy so evil it was life changing on many fronts.

Lives to be affected and be changed forever that day. So many peoples lives had been touched by the story of a young girl who's life was nothing short of brutal torture for years. The Battles she'd would have to face after one tragedy ended and others had began. The pain of healing day by day would prove to be torture.

(Chapter 18)

(Healing)

Having to face other tragedies along her way in life. It just seemed unfair to place one person under so much pressure. It was nothing short of a miracle that she has made it as far as she has through life unto this day. The heavy burdens that Sue still carries to this very day. I am so happy we still have her here with us.

Today she still lives and prospers living in peace finally. she has gone through so many tests in life. She is only one of many survivors that have had to live the torture of being sexually molested. I feel the law should be changed to punish offenders to the fullest extent of the law. And that it should be no less than a life sentence. In order to save any others from being hurt.

So many people get away with all of the hurt they place upon others. And others who get caught often get nothing more than a slap on the hand depending on which state you live in the law varies from state to state. Leaving so many people and families without justice. And that is the saddest part of it all. The law should be way more tougher than they are.

I've had to live a part of my life with this fear. I'd learned to keep it all a secret for years. Never being able to ever fully heal inside. Causing me to choose many bad choices in my life. Not being able to hold a steady job. Living in constant depression. Battling my soul for survival. Overcoming several addictions to many different drugs as well as Alcohol.

Not being able to enjoy the things in life I once enjoyed. When this kind of crime is played out on someone they are never the same anymore after that. Their life becomes a hurricane on daily basis. The choices they make are most often the wrong ones. It's as if the choices are made most often. And it is known that their not the right choice but still made anyway.

There should be more support networks for people to reach out to for help. A lot of people end up not being able to find their way back from these incidents and end up taking their own lives. And that is a sad picture to paint. That's how bad the situation can become if help is not received in some cases.

(Chapter 19)

(Hope)

I have been in a relationship personally with a woman for 7 years. Who has gone through this kind of hell. And so I get to witness the damage first hand. The nightmares that wake her up at night sometimes crying sometimes scared to death. Shaking like a leaf as if she's going through it allover again. That very same situation. I can sometimes hear her pleading for help while she sleeps.

Clearly shaken still to this day from the tragedies of her childhood. Things that most people in life couldn't begin to even fathom. Things that would cause a normal person to end up suicidal. From what

I've witnessed living with another who has faced these same problems. Can be one hell of a battle to just live in a normal relationship.

Is that they are so strong willed. Survivors of the worst possible happenings in life. The strength these people carry is something that is unexplainable. They usually are the people who have a beautiful heart and love and care about everyone. Those who often are givers and not takers. They'd rather give than to receive. That is a huge part of what keeps them ticking.

They usually are the givers in life who would hand over his or her shirt to another if they needed it. The most wonderful people I've met are those who have suffered. Been humbled by life. And still have the power to be able to love others without judgement. Well that is just a thing of beauty all on its own.

To be able to wake up each day and be grateful for another day in life. That's the kind of people victims usually end up to be from what I've learned and seen from them in my years on this earth. It's eye opening to see that much torment happen to someone. But in the end only to make them stronger as a human being as they go on with their life.

(Chapter 20)

(Others)

I have seen many others who have had this happen to them as well. They go on to live their lives but in fear as they go. Never to be fully able to live normal again. Always in defensive mode in all they do. Especially when they are in an area they are not familiar with or at night as well. Trust becomes the number one issue in an abused person's life.

My sister had to live this way for many years after becoming a teenager and was almost abducted as a teenager as well but in our own home town. Luckily that day myself and others had been there playing football. We were having fun and not paying any attention to the girls who at the time were going up and into the woods. Which they weren't supposed to do.

That's when it happened. A man had grabbed my sister up and started to molest her right smack in the woods of Water Works Park. The local neighborhood park where we lived. There was a set of woods directly on the left side of the football field. And there was a split section of woods and tracks there also. The Railroad ran that section heavily during the day hours. But it was slow on the weekends.

So luckily I had heard screams coming from the woods. I just didn't know it was my sister until she had came running out of the woods yelling and screaming at the top of her lungs. Scared to death as she ran towards our direction at the football field. I looked her way and immediately ran her way. As I ran I yelled for her to keep running my way.

It was at that exact moment a weird looking guy had also came out of the woods also but he was riding a ten speed bicycle. She pointed him out immediately and the chase was on. My friends and I tried to chase the man down only to be out ran by the bike. And the pervert riding it who was now scared for his life for the most part.

My sister after it was all over with was clearly shaken and the police were called. They never did find the man not even a clue led them in any certain direction. That's how fast a situation can arise. And if one is not careful they can find themselves in a situation they can't get out of. Maybe to even end up kidnapped or killed. Never to bee seen alive again by their loved ones.

It happens to often in the world we live in. Women and children getting attacked sexually assaulted sometimes even murdered by the suspect. It needs to be addressed more than it is. The world has become so violent. So violent that crimes that happen these days seem so minimal. Almost as if Its just a regular occurrence anymore.

(Chapter 21)

(Change)

It had been learned that Shirley had been raped since she was ten years old and was scared to say anything to anyone. The thoughts constantly churned her through mind. If I tell I die. For years she had to live with that threat running through her mind. I couldn't believe that she had been forced to suffer for that long.

I feel as if on that day the Lord had stepped in and enforced his will to be done in order to save Shirley from any more torture than she had already endured. If not, this may have not stopped for many more years after. And it had been going on for a long damn time. To long for any child to have to bear the fear of that horrible situation on their own.

I often wondered how long would it have gone on if grandma hadn't came home from work and witnessed the attack on her own daughter when she did. It was the will of the lord that put this to a stop I believe. He'd seen one of his own being defiled and stepped In and took command of the situation. Giving him a taste of his own destruction.

Even though Ellen was placed in prison I believe she would have handled it the same way if given the chance once again I know I probably would have. I can't say I'd of handled it any more different than she had. I don't think anyone I know would have handled it any differently than my grandmother had.

Any father who can do things like that to his own children. Should be ready for those kinds of things to happen to him as well. That's the way I look at things anymore. Life is so brutal to some people and for reasons I'll never know. Life sometimes just isn't very fair to those who are pure souls. They are the ones who seem to suffer the most and I never could understand just exactly why they carried that burden.

(Chapter 22)

(Outlook)

Some say it's the work of the devil. Others would say it's just life and only the strong survive. And some would say that it's the lords will. It just don't seem fair to me. Something as fragile as a child being abused doesn't sit right with me at all. The world can be a sick and twisted place in which to live sometimes.

I feel like people should be prosecuted to the fullest when committing crimes like this against children. It's happened to so many people I know. And they grow into adults that just can't seem to find their way In life no matter how hard they try. Something always seems to bring the past back to haunt them.

Turning to a world of Drugs or Alcohol to kill the pain Inside. Most stay sheltered in their homes. Away from other people because their afraid to even interact with others. Living a minimal life at best. Always wondering why ? why would God allow this to happen to me ? That is the one question that is most often asked by a victim.

To them it seems like everyone and everything have turned their backs on them. Feeling hopeless and helpless along their way In life. Not knowing in which way to turn. Who to turn to and who to confide in. During their time of need who to trust is the biggest difficulty. Trust issues being the date left behind from the abuse.

(Chapter 23)

(Fear)

Scared to trust anyone ever again. They also struggle to make proper decisions In life. So many things change for a person who has gone through abuse. I've been there done that so. I know what it feels like to have things done to you personally. I suffered from abuse for so many years myself.

It's the moment you let it all out that you become free. Being able to let it all go once and for all. That's the moment one can start to heal inside. It's how I learned to heal myself. Over the years I had this madness running inside of me. I could never escape it fully. It would come back and haunt me many times.

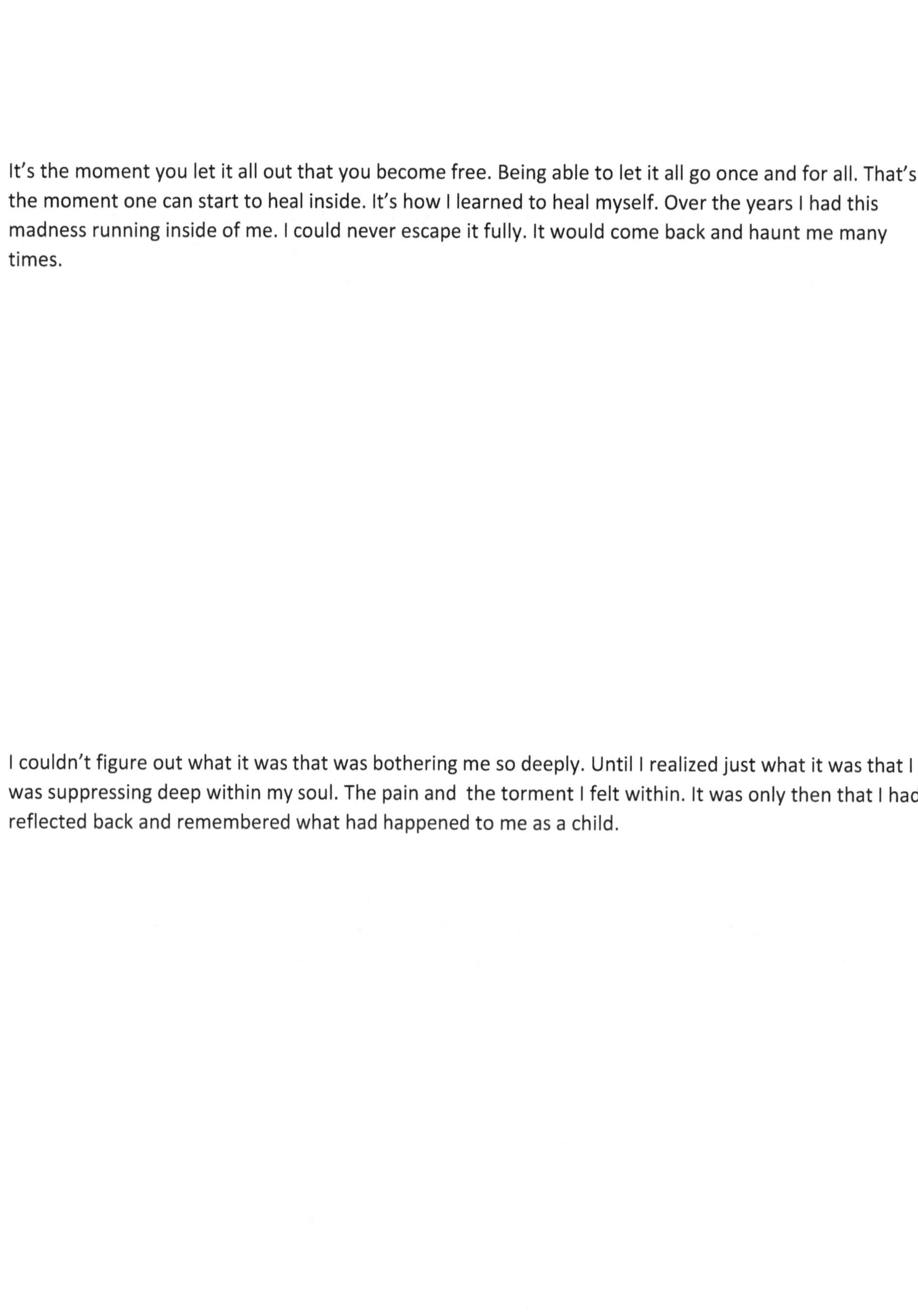

I couldn't figure out what it was that was bothering me so deeply. Until I realized just what it was that I was suppressing deep within my soul. The pain and the torment I felt within. It was only then that I had reflected back and remembered what had happened to me as a child.

Then and only then I decided to let go of all of the pain I had pushed aside for so many years. The healing began as I learned how to deal with the issues at hand. All of a sudden the memories would all came rushing back to me once again out of nowhere it seemed. Why was this happening to me ? What was causing these memories to keep on re-occuring.

I had to move forward with the truth. I told my family members what had happened to me. Which shocked them all deeply. But it was a now or never situation. I had just turned 30 years old when I decided to tell it all. It would cause a family war for several years. The entire family stopped talking to one another.

(Chapter 24)

(Healing)

In deciding to write this short book about the murder that took place down in Barboursville Kentucky. It was a healing moment for me. But I also wanted to get this out there for my mother's sister Shirley. She never deserved any of those things that had happened to her. The question though was why had her father done this to her.

After everyone in our family had realized just what it was that she had gone through we were all hurt by it. After all she was family. And had been through a horrible tragedy in her life. Having to be in that room that day. To not only be abused once again. But also having to watch the horrible murder of her father as it all unfolded, was even more damaging to her.

To watch her father get stabbed 28 times or more. And by the hands of her own mother who had committed the horrible act itself. To help free her of being hurt anymore. No more torture no more pain. No more acts of violence being done towards her any longer. The key to it all would be the loss of her mother for 20 years. Their relationship being stripped from them both.

It was just a damn shame that Ellen had been put in prison for saving her own daughter from being molested by her father. Being locked up for 20 years for protecting your own family. Having to go through mandatory electric shock therapy treatments in a mental facility later on down the road. And on a daily basis she would go through pure hell.

Ellen was the one who'd end up being placed in such an awful place. A place for crazy people to live while receiving treatment. Shock therapy on the brain was the new and current treatment Ellen would go through. There was no way to describe the pain she was going through. There was without a doubt a whole lot of agony in going through these procedures.

(Chapter 25)

(Under The Bus)

Basically torture was what she was going through and on a daily basis. No reason for it at all she wasn't crazy she had just killed a man in self defense of her daughter. To keep her from being molested, or Raped whichever you prefer calling it. There wasn't a moment where one could decide rationally on what to do in that short of a time frame.

Which choice to make and make correctly. A crime being committed and in the heat of the moment a mother acting in defense of her daughter. No one could see why any judge would hand down such an awful sentence on a person. For protecting her own child from sexual and mental abuse. It was so easy to see it had been done in defense of a crime.

I feel that's why after her release she'd moved back down to Kentucky. In order to lay low and to stay hidden from the press as well. She just wanted her life back. That's all that she wanted was to be left alone. Finally once and for all. She'd been through a lifetime of hell and torment. And at such an early age in life she would have to learn how to be a survivor.

And yet somehow she had managed to make it through 20 years in Marysville prison for women. And then having been forced into treatment at a mental facility as well. Being instantly forced to partake in Electro Shock Therapy also. Which was by far from normal after all. She wasn't crazy, she'd just snapped in the heat of the moment. In the defense of her daughter.

It was a wonder grandma didn't come out of that facility with brain damage. She'd made it home after all those years of hell and suffering. So many of life's moments would be missed. While being locked away from everyone she had known and loved. In the beginning she would have many visits. But over the years the visits would fade slowly to none.

(Chapter 26)

(Forgotten)

It felt as if she was being totally forgotten by all of her family and friends from the bar she worked at. She had worked so hard for her family to have all that they needed. And yet still life would take her in the wrong direction at the end of it all. Totally stripping her of any life that she'd once had. Leaving any chance of happiness looking to be almost hopeless as well.

Left to suffer for over two decades with only limited contact of family. Having to work and slave for the prison staff. It's a wonder she didn't attempt suicide at some point during her sentence. She showed so much strength and resilience. She had become a survivor there was no doubt about it at all. She would make it out of that Hell Hole.

Just by being able to walk out of Marysville prison on her own two feet. The woman was a different kind of soul there was no doubt. Everyone thought she was ruined and had nothing left to live for. But she had Challis to live for and her dogs her 4 pit bulls. That she loved and adored as if they were her own children. Her extended family of loved ones.

The only thing she would do towards the end of her life was save money. As much as she possibly could. Every where in the house she was leaving her kids something behind for when she left and she surely did do so. From the pillow cases to the cupboards and even inside the mattresses. Money was hidden everywhere inside of the house.

It was when She became sick that Challis could no longer care for her he'd said to my mother. He had told her during the visit that Ellen would tell Challis to just leave her be. That she could take care of herself. And out of fear of being hurt himself. He'd just leave her alone and all by herself. She would have to take care of herself.

Poor ass excuse if you ask me. He should have stood up and told her that he was her husband and it was his job to take care of her. And then he should have cooked for her or had someone else come and do it. He was just a tightwad with his money. Always stashing it away for a later date inside the house somewhere. Most likely for the sake of his own children.

(Chapter 27)

(Money Everywhere)

He allowed her checks to be hers. But he'd only pay the basic bills and stash the rest of his money also. He thought in the end he'd just keep all of the money laying around to himself. What he never planned on was my mother and Shirley coming back down to check on their mother. Making sure that she was being taken care of correctly.

They were not going to allow him to just simply walk away with their mothers money. Especially after he'd let her lay in filth. When they had arrived they'd found their mother laying in her own feces and urine. Bed sores were now all over her body. Mostly from being neglected. Being left to lay in her own piss and shit for days on end at a time.

A simple case of neglect of a human being. The dogs were better cared for than Poor Ellen was. It was easy to see. The authorities had no problem with mom and Shirley taking their mother out of that hell hole once and for all. And gave the OK for them to take her back up North and out of Kentucky for proper medical treatment.

But by this time it was a little bit to late. There was no way she'd survive being this sick the doctors said. She had developed Pneumonia along the way home and had arrived back in Cincinnati in bad shape. They were worried that Septic shock would come next. She was now upgraded to Critical condition once inside of the emergency room.

The poor woman had bed sores from her head to her toes. Infection had set in her body as well. She was not going to make it very long being in the shape she was in now. Dorothy and Shirley were told to prepare for the worst. And to tell the family of her condition. That now the infection had also moved into her blood stream as well.

(Chapter 28)

(Neglected)

Ellen Howard had put up the God fight. But in the end her age and her health would take and carry her on out of this world. It was a shame that she'd been so neglected for all that time. Being left alone to fend for herself. While Challis worked on whatever money making opportunities that would come his way. My Grandmother would be left all by herself.

She most likely felt so alone towards the end of her days. Feeling hopeless helpless until Dorothy and Shirley had arrived finally. To try and help their mother recover from her illness. Taking her back home with them. In order to get her proper medical care for her many wounds that now covered her poor old mangled body.

Getting visits from her grandkids she had never met until that final moment. Making her feel so good to finally see them all at one time. It gave her new hope to fight for she would say. But she was so deathly sick at this point. Recovery would be nothing short of a miracle for her. She was hanging on barely by a thread at this point.

In the end she wouldn't make it. Septic Shock would be what took her life so suddenly. After all of the hard work the girls had put in trying to clean the house up and having their mother taken back home with them. To receive care from one of the best hospitals around. Even the top notch care that she'd received hadn't been nearly enough to save her.

The girls were cleaning the house up for Challis out of the kindness of their hearts. They knew he had done all he could for Ellen especially after finding out about his current health conditions with his heart. The whole situation was just awful. The worst part of it all was knowing he was trying to keep all of the money that had been hidden all around the house. Saving it for his own children's best interests.

The two sick people husband and wife trying to make it in life. While both were sick as dogs barely even living their lives due to their health. No help from the outside at all. No kids or grand kids pitching in to help them. So the question that remained was why give it to the kids ? Especially if they hadn't helped them in anyway with his wife's condition ?

(Chapter 29)

(Blessings In Disguise)

It was a blessing when Ellen's two daughters had arrived to help her. To come and check on her all the way from Ohio. It was out of love alone that made them take the journey down home so their mother could see the two of them together and give her somewhat of a huge relief. Knowing that she would be taken care of from that moment forward.

That they had come down to help their mother with the house. It had been so many years since they had all seen each other. It would he a cheerful moment in time long overdue for all of them. They had all been through so much in their lives. More than their fair share for sure. He'll and torment was all they'd known at this point. Life had been a son of a bitch for them all.

So many years of torment and hell they'd all lived but in different lives. They were all survivors for sure. Over coming all of the obstacles that were laid before them all. Their mother had raised them right. The 13 years she'd spent with them raising them to be women. The hard work the pain and anguish that had been suffered. Because of one particular asshole.

Shirley had made it and had some kind of life out in Colorado. And Dorothy had made a life for her self in Cincinnati, Ohio. She had got married and had a huge family of 7 in total. Which her mom was very proud of both her daughters for managing their lives in a good manner. While dealing with abusing, and cheating Jack asses that tried to rule them each and every day.

Becoming a woman and a mother to 5 children in all. Shirley had become a role model for the young out their who had been through such a tragedy. So severe and still somehow through it all had managed to find a way to self persevere through all of it. She was still in the fight for a normal life. She had came up with a possible solution or so she thought. But would have to act on it soon.

(Chapter 30)

(Starting Over)

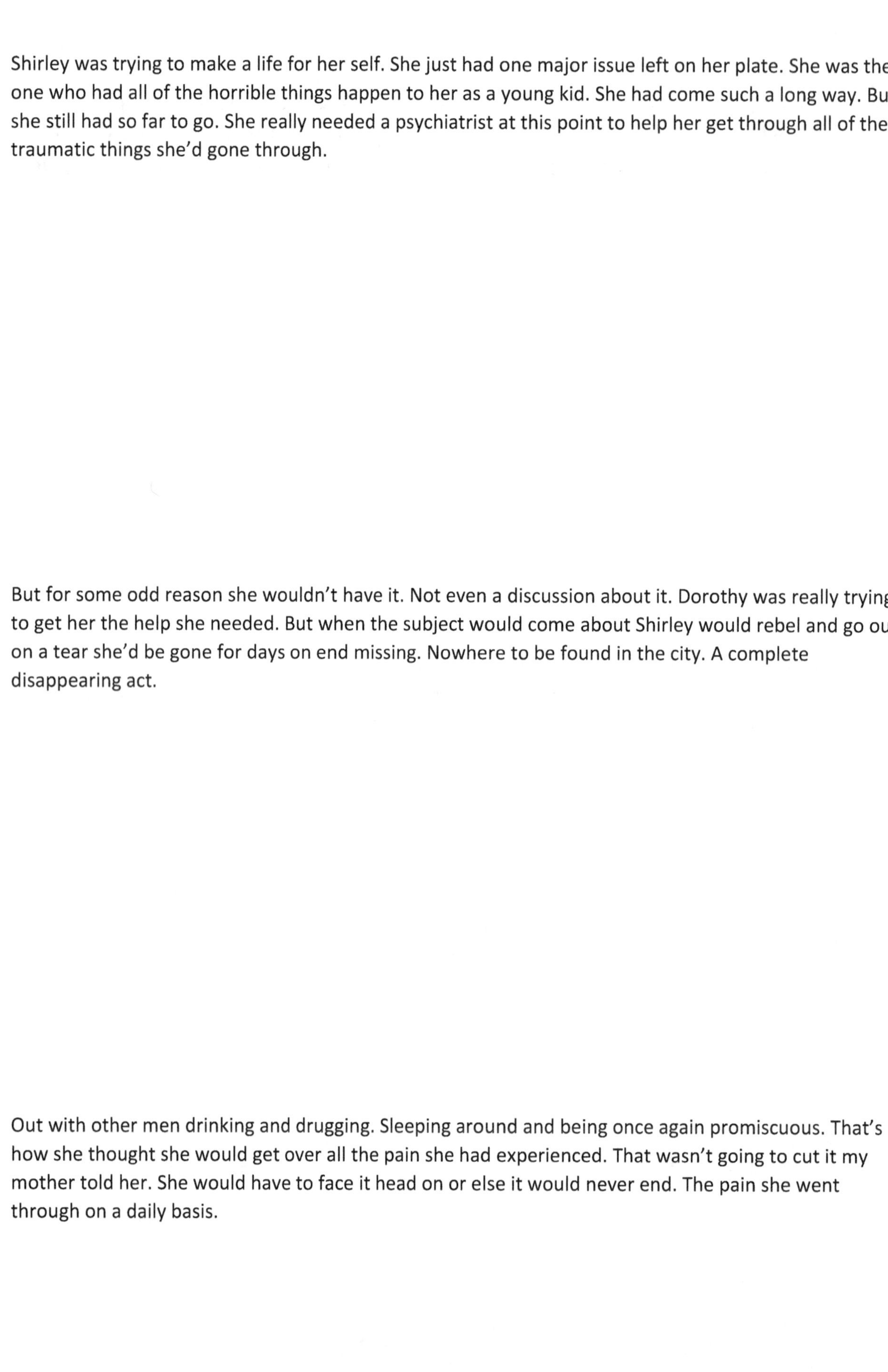

Shirley was trying to make a life for her self. She just had one major issue left on her plate. She was the one who had all of the horrible things happen to her as a young kid. She had come such a long way. But she still had so far to go. She really needed a psychiatrist at this point to help her get through all of the traumatic things she'd gone through.

But for some odd reason she wouldn't have it. Not even a discussion about it. Dorothy was really trying to get her the help she needed. But when the subject would come about Shirley would rebel and go out on a tear she'd be gone for days on end missing. Nowhere to be found in the city. A complete disappearing act.

Out with other men drinking and drugging. Sleeping around and being once again promiscuous. That's how she thought she would get over all the pain she had experienced. That wasn't going to cut it my mother told her. She would have to face it head on or else it would never end. The pain she went through on a daily basis.

It's not how you fix what happened to you she told Shirley time and time again. The next time the subject would be brought up she would take off once again. This time back to Colorado she'd go. And the plan was to not ever come back again. Not even to visit on holidays. That was he next plan. Which was a horrible issue in itself.

Charlie had been gone for a few years now passed and gone to heaven. Her ne would be brought up sometimes at the table at breakfast or dinner. The wild antics she would pull while she was drinking during her visits to see us. She was very lucky that my mother loved her and knew what she'd gone through. Or she would have beat her ass herself.

(Chapter 31)

(Change)

Things would change over the years. Never to be the same again. We missed them but everyone had their own lives now. Everyone had learned how to manage their lives finally. My mother would concentrate on her own family as she raised her children into responsible adults. She had raised her kids to be kind and loving. But also to take no shit from anyone ever.

Dad had done went and had a stroke on us. Now we were all pitching in to take care of him. I was working with a Tree Service outfit and had to work 6 days a week. The business was booming for us. I would crawl in the door most of the time at dusk. Totally exhausted from the hard labor my job required from me. Ken Helms Tree Service was my new way of life.

Very hard work I must say. We had so many customers. Usually working 6 or 7 days a week. Going fishing maybe one day a week if I were lucky. I was making great money but had no time to spend it on anything. So drugs it was for me. It's when the key was turned and I walked through the door to addiction. And that journey for me was pure hell.

And so the battle would begin for my life and my soul. Trying to keep the devil out. It was when I really decided to maybe break free from the pain that I was keeping locked inside my soul. All of the bad things that happened to me as a child. I couldn't figure out how to release my demons. Letting them go finally for good. So I could start the healing process myself.

It would be a few years down the road before I would let loose all of my secrets to my family members. Finally freeing my self of all of the torment. All of the hell I'd gone through as well. It would split the family apart but it had to be known. I had let it all go while I was doing time for child support once again. As I'd done so many other times before.

(Chapter 32)

(Freedom)

Id come to the realization that I had to cleanse my soul. So I could be free and start to learn how to live once again without having anything holding me back from what it was I was trying to accomplish in life. And only then could I be able to try and start to be a man. And living my life as a normal human being once again after all of the years that I had missed out on.

Years of chaos and mayhem that had gone on in my early years as a young kid. Would keep me trapped for many years. It wasn't until I met my long lost family members that I would be able to muster the courage to let it all go. As I sat in that dirty cold ass jail cell. Being strung along as if I were a puppet. I had become angry and enraged all of a sudden.

Id finally realized that it was time to take charge of my life and do what it was that was necessary for me to come face to face with those who hurt me growing up. It was then that I'd do so and break free and eventually find my way through my journey in life. Whether it was a good one or a bad one it had to be traveled somewhere, somehow.

And now that I have I've found a whole new life of adventure that I can open up and share with the public and the rest of the world. Finally being set free to live life my way. The way that I would choose to live it for once. Doing the things that I love to do. Fishing and hunting also camping in the forest across Ohio, Kentucky and Indiana.

Opening a new world to me without violence. Only peace being allowed to come in to my life. I found my calling I had only hoped that all of my other family members had learned how to do the same thing. It took a lot of things happening for me to be able to see the light. Once I seen it though on that day it was clear to me.

(Chapter 33)

(The Light)

Id only wondered if they had seen the light themselves. I'd hoped that Shirley had found a way to move on and move forward in her life. After all if anyone deserved the good life it was her. The poor thing had been through all of those horrible things in her early youth. When she was supposed to be growing up. Having fun as children are supposed to.

My mother had always tried to guide her to the positive side of life and keep her their. But she would rebel so many times and take off on her. Only to crash and burn in the end. Not ever realizing what others were trying to help her do. They were trying to help her through the tough times of her life.

Shirley had always thought that others were trying to sabotage her in life. She didn't trust anyone at all. And who could blame her. After all she had been through as a child. That's why it took so long for her to be able to live somewhat of a normal life. The deep pain couldn't be tamed for a long time.

The reason she had moved so far away to Colorado. Was to escape all of her childhood memories. Once and for all she would go so far away from home. And be comfortable being several states away from her family. She thought the pain would just go away. But it were never going to be that easy of a task.

It was the same with Charlie. She had moved all the way up to Michigan to get away from her home town of Kentucky. But the one thing neither of them could escape was the pain. That would be impossible to do until the reason for all of that pain had been let go. Only then would their even be a hint of a chance to overcome it all.

That would be apparent and would let itself show when they'd visit us and stay intoxicated during their whole visit. My mother couldn't believe it. How they were acting in front of all of us kids. She had never seen women get that drunk ever in her life time. She'd seen men act that way but never women though.

(Chapter 34)

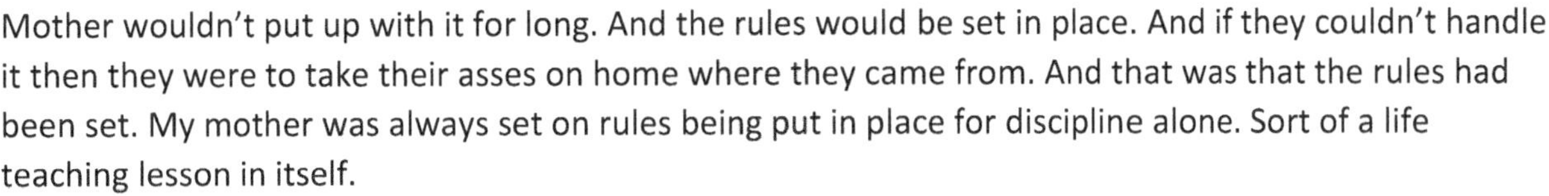

(Memories)

Mother wouldn't put up with it for long. And the rules would be set in place. And if they couldn't handle it then they were to take their asses on home where they came from. And that was that the rules had been set. My mother was always set on rules being put in place for discipline alone. Sort of a life teaching lesson in itself.

If they couldn't follow the rules oh well that was that they had to go home. My mother wasn't going to deal with it. She loved her sisters and missed them very much. But she wasn't going to have them drunk in her home and acting fools. She already had enough to deal with. Her own asshole husband would take care of that all on his own accord.

After all she had enough on her plate already. Dealing with my drink father coming in drunk every night and showing his ass. She wanted them to see how it was to be sober and deal with a drunk. Maybe then they would see the light and sober up she hoped. She couldn't guide them anymore than that. Even if they looked at her to be a bitch. She couldn't help it.

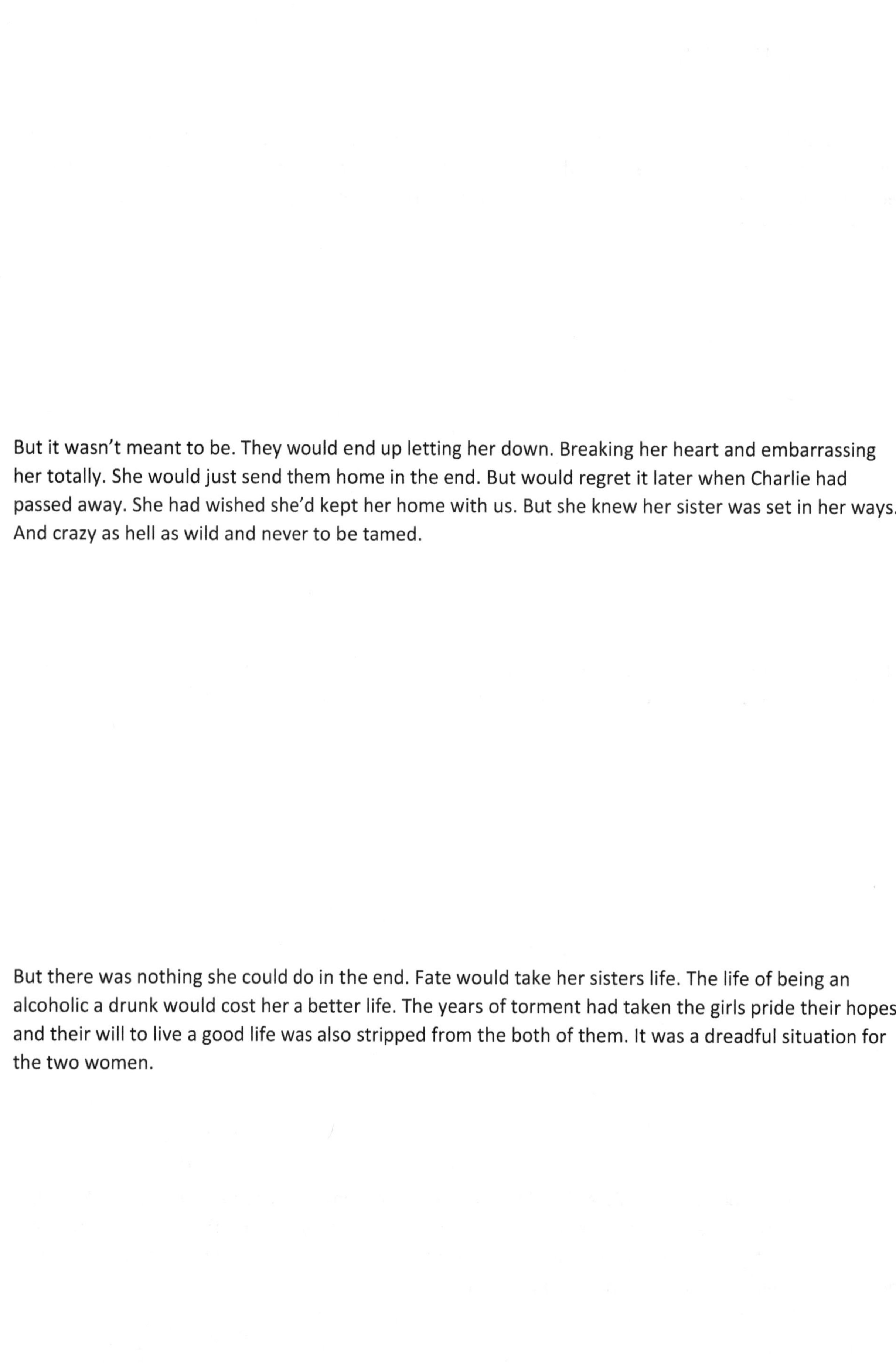

But it wasn't meant to be. They would end up letting her down. Breaking her heart and embarrassing her totally. She would just send them home in the end. But would regret it later when Charlie had passed away. She had wished she'd kept her home with us. But she knew her sister was set in her ways. And crazy as hell as wild and never to be tamed.

But there was nothing she could do in the end. Fate would take her sisters life. The life of being an alcoholic a drunk would cost her a better life. The years of torment had taken the girls pride their hopes and their will to live a good life was also stripped from the both of them. It was a dreadful situation for the two women.

(Chapter 35)

(unhappy endings)

In the end No one would be able to attend Charlie's funeral in Michigan. Which broke my mother's heart. Shirley didn't even make it. To far away to even try to get there. Life was happening to people and they couldn't break away long enough to make it. Dorothy carried tons of guilt for missing her sisters funeral.

We never seen Shirley ever again. She was wrapped up in her own misery still wasting her life away moment by moment. The alcohol and the drugs controlling her life. And she would never heal enough to have a normal relationship with her kids. Even though she would reach out and attempt it several times. The long distance calls were never accepted.

My mother the glue that had tried to hold it all together for so many years would get sick. Ending up with pancreatic cancer by the time she had found out that she had it. The doctors were way late finding the cancer It had hidden well. It was now to late to do anything for her. She was given a death sentence and that would be that in a nutshell so to speak.

All they could do was medicate her to the fullest of there capabilities. The woman was so sick and so scared. She didn't want to leave her children behind. As she left slowly for heaven. Her kids all gathered by her side for the last months of her life. Staying by her side day and night. As she would carry on while in pain and misery. Cussing like a storm trooper caught up in a blizzard.

To watch their mother go was so Traumatic for them. But they knew once she'd pass away there would be no more suffering for her. She would be at the gates of heaven finally. With her children and her husband. They had already passed away and were waiting for her up in heaven.

(Chapter 36)

(Dorothy's passing)

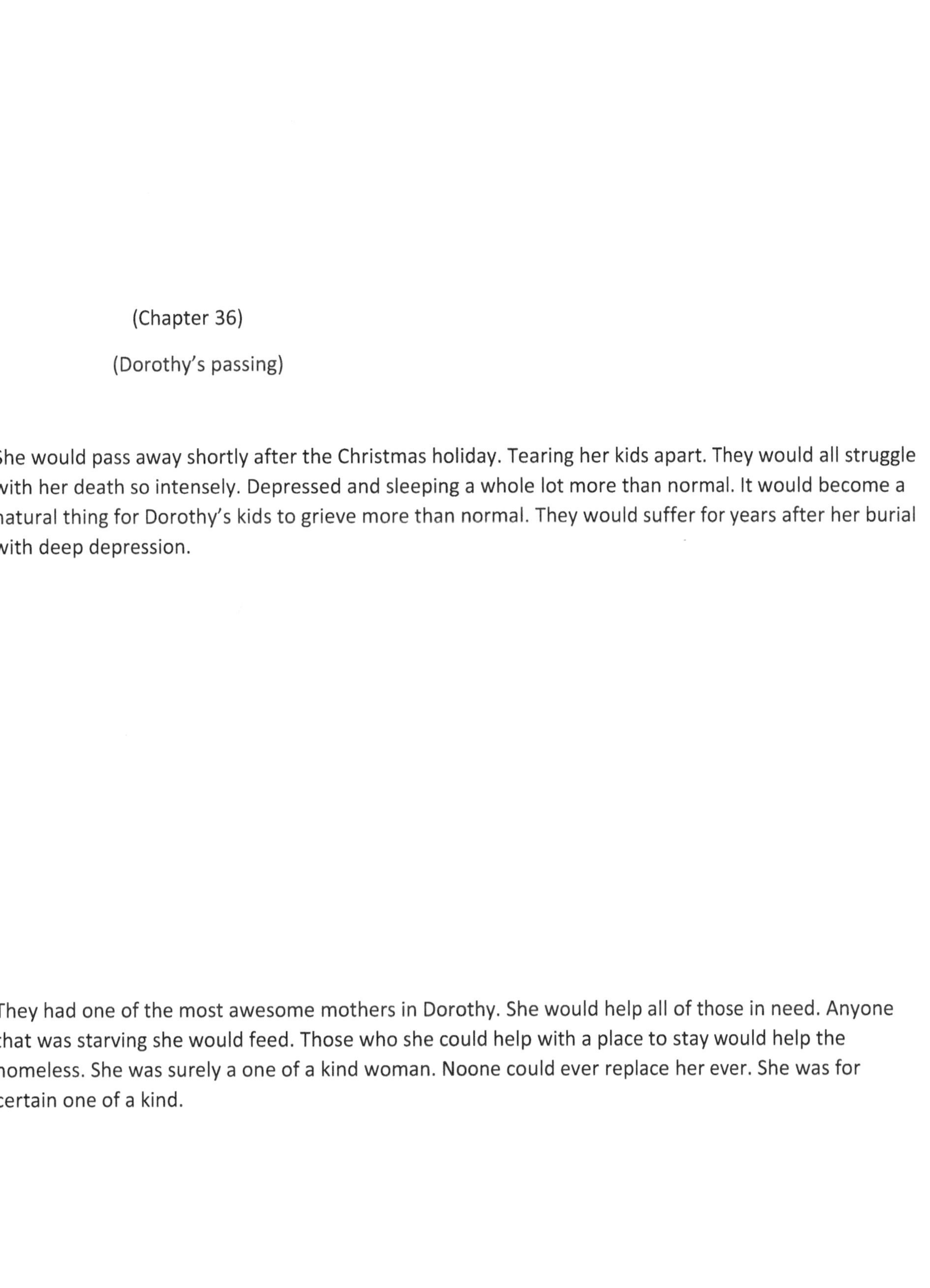

She would pass away shortly after the Christmas holiday. Tearing her kids apart. They would all struggle with her death so intensely. Depressed and sleeping a whole lot more than normal. It would become a natural thing for Dorothy's kids to grieve more than normal. They would suffer for years after her burial with deep depression.

They had one of the most awesome mothers in Dorothy. She would help all of those in need. Anyone that was starving she would feed. Those who she could help with a place to stay would help the homeless. She was surely a one of a kind woman. Noone could ever replace her ever. She was for certain one of a kind.

Irreplaceable in her children s eyes. They would all fall apart for a while after she had passed away. They were lost souls trying to find their way once again. A tragic story for the whole family. But that's how it has been told from the very start of it all. From beginning to the end the full truth of the story. Their lives front and center.

From the murder that had taken their father from them so many years ago. To the tragedy of also losing their mother as well at that same moment in time. The roads they would travel along their each individual journey's in their lives. And the constant Hell and the sacrifices they would endure for so damn long.

Once again meeting again later in their lives. Trying to patch up their pasts along the way. Trying to have a relationship again as sisters only to fail once again. To many traumatic memories to recover from. They were all to stubborn to put up with one another. Those were the cold hard facts of it all.

(Chapter 37)

(Try Again)

They would try and try again to be a family but drugs and alcohol would get in the way. Just as it did in Dorothy's marriage. To many other substances standing in the way of happiness. And would probably keep them from happiness until their deaths. That was the cold hard truth. And it was known to the lot of them.

Life would seem to be nothing but a nightmare for them all. Time and time again bad things would happen tragedy after tragedy. Never giving up fully they would all try to push forward from the Horrors they had faced as kids. The tragedies that had split them all up. Other tragedies bringing them back together from time to time.

Flat out stubbornness always taking them away from the comfort of one another's company. For so many years they would be apart from each other. Not being able to help each other during the years of growing up. When they needed to be able to be their for one another it just wasn't ever possible. And that was the sad part of it all.

All of the girl moments they would have to go through without each other as sisters would greatly torment them also. Upon meeting again so many years later they would have mixed emotions. All of the memories from the past would also come back to haunt them. But the live they had for one another was very deep.

(Starting Over)

They would have to learn allover again how to suppress the past and live for the future. All 3 of them. But they knew it wouldn't last. For once they went their separate ways once again the memories of their horrific past would come back and haunt them all once again.

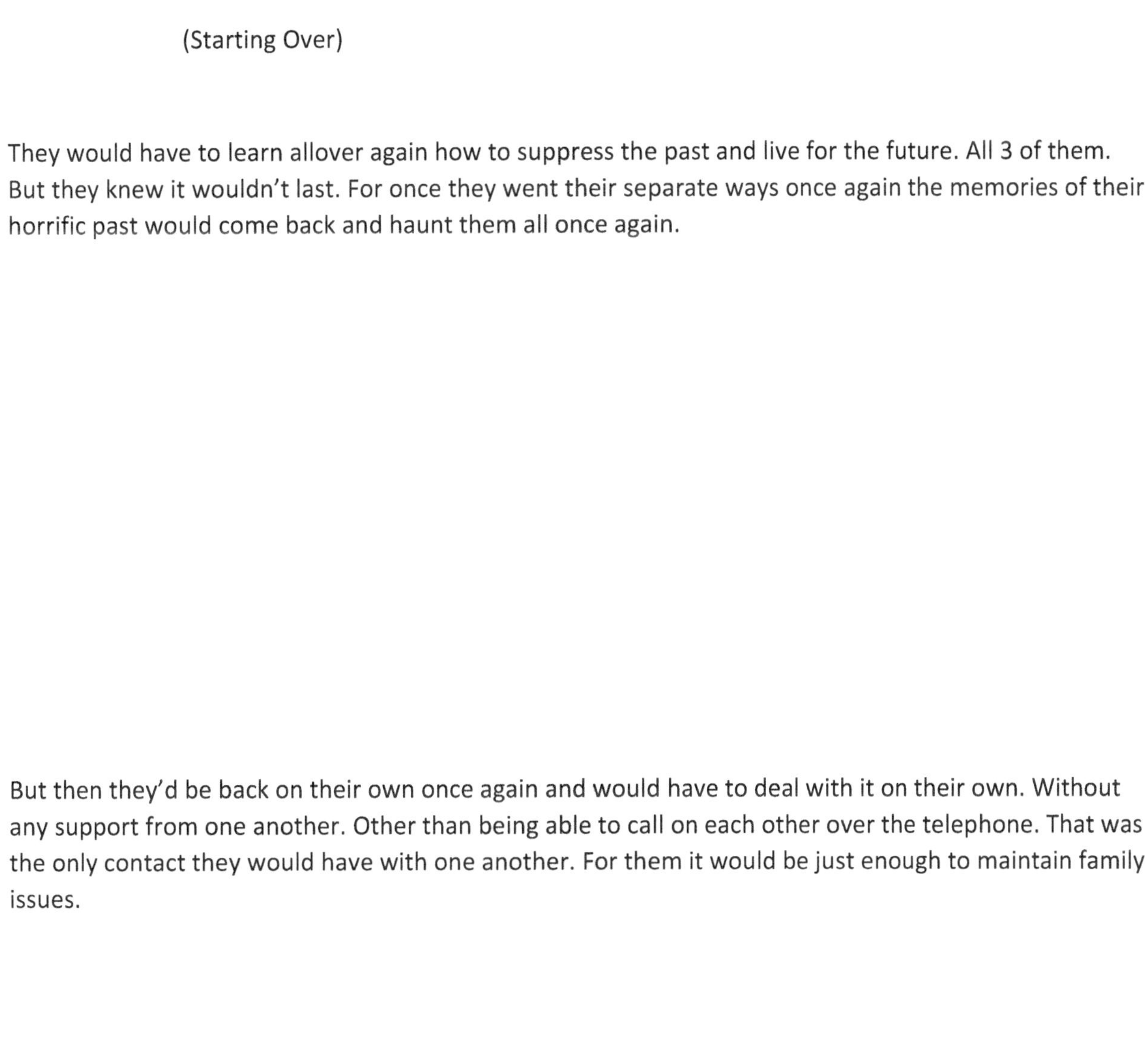

But then they'd be back on their own once again and would have to deal with it on their own. Without any support from one another. Other than being able to call on each other over the telephone. That was the only contact they would have with one another. For them it would be just enough to maintain family issues.

When Dorothy passed away it only left Shirley standing on her own. She could contact her daughter. But that probably wouldn't go down well. Ashley would end up raising ten kinds of hell when that moment happened. She resented her mother for leaving her behind. They all had felt that way in some sort of way.

And she would probably ly never get over it either. She had only known Dorothy as her mother. And she was treated very well by her stepmother. She was really down when she had passed away. She'd quit her job and slept a whole lot too. The only mother she'd known was now gone and in heaven.

Like the rest of her kids did. It was a horrible moment for them all. They couldn't get passed it. To many lost in such a short period of time. And it would take years to get over. So much death in such a short amount of time. It had got the best of Jeff for sure for quite a while after their deaths.

He would try to take his own life by way of overdose. Only to fail yet once again. He'd tried it before a long ways back many years before all of the new tragedy that had taken place as of late. He was now mad at the work and the Lord also. Not understanding exactly what the reason was for taking all 3 of them and doing so as fast as it had happened.

(Chapter 39)

(Madness)

Jeff would struggle severely for several long months after laying his mother to rest. On top of a huge hill at the cemetery. The day a very cold one indeed. Jeff was numb that day and stayed that way for months after he left her on that hill. He now struggled with his own sanity now. In a battle to keep the will to stay alive were the new war being fought.

Would he win or lose ? That was the new question that everyone including his own sisters had wondered about. He was really struggling to understand why all of this had happened to his family. So many questions ran through the man's mind now. He stayed depressed for a very long time. Not knowing what to do with his life.

Until one day he had sat down in a empty and dark room. Only a small candle had given light to the room. He though long and hard about everything. He then came to the conclusion that he would tell their story. Leaving the legacies of his family members who were now with the lord. It was in that moment he had figured out his path.

He would stay busy for the next several months. Writing out his families stories of suffering and survival. The true events that had taken place and also had shaped all of their lives. Binding them together as a whole. A family with a strong and united front. Their love for one another so strong. Being there for each other through all of the pain as well as their suffering.

It would all finally be told years after my Grandmother's death. Just exactly why the district attorney had set out to get such a steep sentence against her. When she had killed her husband she had committed what was called overkill. She hat hit every single organ inside his body upon the 28 stabbings she'd lashed out on her husband.

(Chapter 40)

(DECISIONS)

That had been the one and only reason the court system had set out to give her such a steep sentence. It was such a brutal attack that it had taken the coroner hours in order to sew him back together after they'd finished the autopsy. The cause of death was easily figured out. It was the simple fact that another choice could have been made.

Other than the 28 multiple stab wounds of a defenseless man. Who had no clue the attack was even coming. But the court also had taken into consideration that the father had knowingly caused harm to his own daughter. The sexual abuse as well as the mental and physical abuse also. That was why she wasn't given a life sentence in return for her crime.

Still so many local citizens were highly upset by the sentence that had been handed down. They felt that it was to harsh of a penalty for defending her own family from harms way. That was a well known fact during the fast trial that Ellen had been given. After the fact new laws would be brought about for self defense of those who'd suffered abuse of many kinds.

This whole Story was very traumatizing for me to even sit down as I would attempt to write it and finish it as well. This was a very dark period in life for my whole family and I as well. But I wanted this story to be told. I wanted vindication for my Grandmother who was punished harshly for defending her daughter from a sexual attack.

As she had walked in on the attack itself taking place. I could only imagine what anyone would do if put in that very same situation. I had often placed myself there also. And I came to the conclusion every time. That I would have probably done the damn thing in that situation just as she had done.

(The End)

This book was brought about by The true story about my Grandmother Ellen Howard. Who had been accused of Murder. For walking in and saving her daughter from a sexual assault by her own father. The lives that had been affected in many ways. The tragedies that followed after the sentence was handed down. All true events and without a doubt a gripping and horrific story.

 Written by

Jeffrey David Lilly Jr.

August 1st 2022

Dedicated to my family.